Bento Box Recipes That Will Make You Want More: 30 amazing bento box recipes you must try

Ida Smith

Published by Ida Smith, 2021.

BENTO BOX RECIPES THAT WILL MAKE YOU WANT MORE: 30 AMAZING BENTO BOX RECIPES YOU MUST TRY

First edition. September 28, 2021.

ISBN: 979-8201176976

Written by Ida Smith.

Table of Contents

Introduction

Packing meals in a bento box originated from Japan and since its inception, it has gone viral and the whole world has abducted the bento box method of preserving meals till they are ready to eat. Do you have kids? The bento box will be perfect for packing lunch for your kids and the best part is, the meals can be decorated as you will love it. It is certain that lunchtime is that time of the day when you go grab unhealthy snacks to satisfy your hunger, but with a bento box, you can make quick lunch from home and take it to work so you can eat healthily. In this cookbook, you have 30 cute and tasty recipes to prepare for your bento boxes.

Salmon teriyaki in honey

Salmon is very nutritious seafood and there is no better way to have lunch than to have a healthy meal. It is filling and will save you from eating junk food during lunch.

Preparation Time: 10 minutes

Makes: 1

Ingredients

- 1 piece of salted salmon
- 1 tsp. of soy sauce
- 1 tsp. of honey
- 1 tsp. of mirin
- 1 tsp. of black pepper
- ½ cup of oil

Directions

Heat oil in a pan, and fry your salmon for about 5 minutes, turning each side and remove from pan. Place the soy sauce, mirin, and honey in the pan and stir properly. When it begins to bubble, return the salmon and simmer for another 2 minutes, turning to coat properly.

Sprinkle your black pepper on it, remove and let it cool a bit. Pack in your bento box.

Carrot glazed in honey

Honey glazed carrot is a simple lunch time snack. If you are too lazy to prepare a decent meal, then this is a perfect lunch time snack to pack in your bento box.

Preparation Time: 10 minutes

Makes: 2

Ingredients

- 1 big carrot
- ½ tbsp. of honey
- ½ tsp. of salt
- ½ tsp. of pepper
- 1 tsp. of ground cumin

Directions

Slice your carrot into any shape of your choice and boil until it is tender. Drain the water away; add your honey, salt and pepper, and a little cumin.

Keep stirring until the moisture is evaporated, remove from heat and let it cool a bit, then place in your bento box.

Spicy pepper shrimp

The sound of pepper shrimp will make your tummy rumble because it is tasty and amazing.

Preparation Time: 10 minutes

Makes: 2

Ingredients

- 3 big frozen shrimps
- ½ cup of oil
- ½ tsp. of salt
- ½ tsp. of ground black pepper

Directions

Put a little oil in a pan, add your frozen shrimps and simmer for about 5 minutes. Add your salt and pepper, simmer for another few minutes until it is well cooked.

Allow to cool and place in your bento box.

Bacon wrapped in asparagus

The bacon wrapped in asparagus is an amazing side dish that can be prepared immediately.

Preparation Time: 10 minutes

Makes: 3

Ingredients

- 1 spear of trimmed asparagus
- 1 tsp. of ground black pepper
- 1 pound of bacon
- 2 tbsp. of oil

Directions

Slice your asparagus into equal parts, blanch it in a small saucepan until it is tender but firm. Drain liquid and let it cool. Lay the bacon slices flat, place asparagus on it, wrap firmly using a toothpick to hold it.

Heat oil in a pan, place bacon in it and simmer for about 5 minutes, add pepper and let it cool before placing in your bento box.

Pan-fried mushroom

Pan-fried mushroom or komachibu can serve as the perfect bento box lunch side dish. It is crispy and tasty and can be served with some fruits.

Preparation time: 10 minutes

Makes: 4

Ingredients

- ½ tsp. of sugar
- 1 tbsp. of mirin
- 1 tsp. of soy sauce
- 1 cup of dried shiitake mushroom
- 1 tbsp. of oyster sauce
- 1 cup of komachibu
- 2 cups of water

Directions

Soak your mushroom in 2 cups of water overnight. Soak your komachibu in for just 5 minutes in cold water, remove and drain make sure there is no excess liquid and set aside.

Fill your pan with one cup of mushroom water and set aside the mushroom with the remaining water. Add your komachibu in the mushroom water, add your soy sauce, sugar, oyster sauce, and mirin and let it simmer until the liquid has evaporated.

Mix properly, add your mushrooms and cook for an extra minutes. Remove and serve.

Cheeseburger in bento box

Ever had mini cheeseburgers? Guess what? They are the perfect fit for your bento box. It is something you can quickly put together in the morning, arrange it in your bento box, and enjoy during lunch.

Preparation Time: 20 minutes

Makes: 4

Ingredients

- 1 pound of ground beef
- 1 pound of brown sugar
- 1/3 cup of mustard
- 2 tsp. of shredded cheese
- 2 tbsp. of ketchup
- ½ cup of Worcestershire sauce
- 1 cup of biscuit
- 2 cups of flour

- 2 cups of shortening
- 1/2 cup of baking powder
- 2 tbsp. of milk
- 1 tsp. of salt
- ½ tsp. of pepper

Directions

Preheat the oven to about 400 degrees. Mix your flour with a little salt, add your shortening and baking powder and mix together. Then, gradually pour milk into the flour mixture and knead until it forms smooth dough.

Sprinkle a little flour on your flat surface table, place the dough and roll out until it is smooth, cut into 4 pieces and make it flat. Place in your muffin tray and set aside.

Cook your beef until it is well cooked. Add your other ingredients and cook properly.

Top the beef on the muffin tray add cheese on it and bake for about 15 minutes. When it is golden brown, remove and serve.

Little baby bear shaped rice

This can be made especially for your kids as the rice in form a baby bear's head will excite them.

Preparation Time: 15 minutes

Serves; 2

Ingredients

- ½ tofu skin, fried
- ½ cup of rice
- 2 leaves of lettuce
- 1 small already made meatball
- 1 pack of spaghetti noodle, uncooked
- 1 pack of cooked broccoli florets
- 1 green pea
- 1 piece of nori

Directions

Stuff rice in your tofu skin and place in your bento box. Line the other parts of the box with your lettuce leaves. Slice your meatballs in tiny bits, and attach the spaghetti as a little baby bear's ear and place in the wrapped tofu.

Punch a little hole in the middle of the tofu, place a green pea into it then cut the eyes and a smile from the nori and place on the tofu. And it is ready to be eaten.

Lemon flavored pasta salad

Looking for that perfect summer treat? This recipe is perfect. Pasta salad with lemon and cheese gives you a healthy lunch meal packed in your Bento Box.

Preparation Time: 10 minutes

Makes: 6

Ingredients

- 1 pack of ozro pasta
- 1 pound of roasted pepper
- ½ cup of lemon zest
- ½ cup of fresh basil, chopped
- ½ cup of oil
- 1 tsp. of salt
- 1/3 cup of parsley, fresh

- ½ cup of yellow and red tomatoes, chopped
- 2 green onions, diced
- ½ cup of lemon juice

Directions

Add your pasta to boiling water, add salt and cook for about 10 minutes. Remove from heat, drain and set aside. While your pasta is cooking, mix your lemon zest, lemon juice, and oil in a small bowl.

Put your pasta into the lemon mixture, mix properly and add your veggies. Place in your fridge to cool before dishing into your bento boxes.

Sushi rice stuffed with tofu

Sushi rice stuffed in the pockets of fried tofu is great for lunch and the sweat-salty taste makes it unique and amazing.

Preparation Time: 25 minutes

Makes: 3

Ingredients

- 3 sheets of deep fried tofu
- 1 cup of dashi stock
- 1/3 cup of sugar
- 2 tbsp. of sake
- 2 tbsp. of mirin
- ½ cup of soy sauce
- 3 cups of sushi rice

Directions

Blanch your tofu sheets in boiling water for a few minutes. Drain and let it cool. Slice in half and open up the pockets.

Mix your dashi stock, sake, mirin, sugar, and soy sauce in a pan and allow it to boil. Put your tofu pockets in a pan and simmer for about 20 minutes. Remove from pan, let it cool and stuff it with your rice and the dashi mixture, fold down, and pack in your bento box.

Ham and grilled Cheese

A combination of the cambozola cheese and the black forest ham is what makes this simple lunch unique and it is okay to park it in your bento box for lunch.

Preparation Time: 10 minutes

Makes: 2

Ingredients

- 1 pound of black forest ham
- 1 stick of unsalted butter, sliced
- 2 oz of cambozola cheese, softened
- 2 medium sized diced onions
- 4 slices of rye bread
- 1 tbsp. of oil

Directions

Spread your butter on each slice of the bread and set aside. Heat your oil in a pan, place your bread slices in the pan with the buttered side down. Place your cheese slices, onions and ham on the bread. Cover with the other bread slices, toast for about 5 minutes and serve.

Wheat noodle and meat sauce

Wheat noodles eaten with meat sauce tastes heavenly. It is an amazing lunch that can be prepared within few minutes.

Preparation Time: 15 minutes

Makes: 2

Ingredients

- 3 0z of dried udon noodles
- 1/2 cup of miso peanut meat sauce
- 1 cup of bean sprouts, trimmed
- 1 cucumber, seed removed and thinly sliced
- 3 red radishes sliced
- 1 small green onion, diced

Directions

Cook noodles for about 10 minutes. Remove from heat and drain. Arrange the noodles in your bento box. Boil water in a pan, add your bean sprouts and boil for just 2 minutes, remove and drain.

Put your veggies in another compartment of your bento box, and then put miso peanut meat sauce in another compartment of your bento box, then when you are ready to eat, you eat together.

Taco and shredded chicken

This chicken and tacos can be served with corn tortillas that are healthy. Pack it in your bento box with tomatoes and cucumbers to make it even tastier.

Preparation Time: 10 minutes

Makes: 1

Ingredients

- 1 chicken breast, shredded
- 1 tsp. of cumin powder
- 1 corn tortilla
- ½ tsp. of taco powder
- ½ tsp. of salt
- ½ tsp. of pepper

Directions

Season your shredded chicken with your taco powder, add a little salt to taste and your cumin powder. Fill your tortilla with the shredded chicken, add your pepper, place in your bento box until you are ready to eat it.

Crabmeat and shredded cabbage salad

Crabmeat salad is very crunchy and it will make a good lunch for your bento box.

Preparation Time: 10 minutes

Makes: 1

Ingredients

- 1 cup of cabbage, shredded
- 1/3 tsp. of salt
- 1 tbsp. of rice vinegar
- 1 tsp. of sugar
- ½ cup of crabmeat
- ½ tsp. of black pepper

Directions

Mix the cabbage and your salt together and massage properly with your hands. Squeeze properly to remove moisture from it. Place it in a bowl, add your vinegar and sugar and mix properly.

Add your crabmeat, sprinkle a little pepper on it and pack in your bento box.

Marinade pan-fried chicken

Marinated chicken makes the chicken very tasty and a tasty meal is what you need after a stressful morning. Pack your fried chicken in your bento box with any side dish and enjoy.

Preparation Time: 15 minutes

Makes: 10

Recipe

- 1 pound of chicken meat, sliced into 10
- ½ cup of cooked cornstarch
- ½ cup of gobo
- 1/3 cup of julienned sake, finely chopped
- 1 tbsp. of soy sauce, dark
- 1 tbsp. of grated ginger
- ½ cup of oil

Directions

Put your chicken in a bowl, add your soy sauce, ginger, and sake, place in your refrigerator to chill for 30 minutes. Remove from fridge then add your gobo and cornstarch and massage well with your hands.

Heat oil in a pan then add your mixed chicken, simmer until it becomes crispy and golden brown, remove from oil, place on a paper towel to drain.

Let it cool a bit before packing it into your bento box.

Rice and mushroom

This is a very popular dish during the fall season when a mushroom is in abundance. Use varieties of flavored mushrooms for this meal to get the kind of taste you desire.

Preparation Time: 30 minutes

Makes: 4

Ingredients

- 2 cups of mixed fresh mushrooms, sliced
- 2 tbsp. of soy sauce
- 1 tbsp. of sake
- 1 tbsp. of mirin
- ½ tsp. of salt
- 2 cups of rice

Directions

Place the mushrooms in a bowl, add your soy sauce, sake, mirin, and salt, massage properly with your hands. Place your rice in a cooker add your mushrooms and cook for about 20 minutes or until it is tender

Remove from heat, let it cool a bit and pack in your bento box.

Deep-fried pork

Fried pork paired with cabbage will be suitable for your bento box meal. It is easy to make and it is equally a healthy meal.

Preparation Time: 15 minutes

Makes: 2

Ingredients

- 2 pounds of port cutlets
- 1 cup of panko bread crumbs
- 1 big egg, whisked
- 1 tsp. of salt
- ½ tsp. of pepper
- ½ cup of flour
- 1 cup of peanut oil

Directions

Trim away excess fat from your pork and slice it gently. Season with your salt and pepper and deep the cutlets into flour, egg and bread crumb.

Heat your peanut oil and fry your coated pork cutlet until it is crispy and golden brown. Remove from oil, drain in a paper towel, drain, slice into longer pieces and let it cool before dishing into your bento boxes.

Rice and veggies

This kind of meal is common among the Japanese and anyone can have a taste of it. Even vegetarians can have it because the rice is mixed with lots of veggies.

Preparation Time: 40 minutes

Makes: 4

Ingredients

- 1 medium-sized carrot
- 1 medium-sized carrot burdock root
- 2 shiitake mushrooms, dried
- 2 cups of cooked white rice
- 2 tbsp. of sake
- 1 tbsp. of turnip
- 2 tbsp. of soy sauce
- ½ tsp. of salt

Directions

Soak your shiitake in water one hour before you are ready to make the meal. Remove from water and reserve the liquid. Squeeze out the excess liquid from the shiitake, remove the stem and chop the caps.

Peel your carrot and shred together with the burdock root and turnip. Slice your shiitake, and place all ingredients in a pot and let it boil for about 20 minutes or until the liquid is absorbed.

Steam the rice for about 10 minutes, add the veggies and fluff with a fork, remove and allow to cool for a few minutes.

Pack in your bento box when it is cool.

Ground beef cabbage roll

Cabbage rolls made with beef can be so tasty and can last in your fridge for a long time. It is easy to make and stress-free.

Preparation Time: 30 minutes

Makes: 2

Ingredients

- 10 cabbage leaves
- 1 small onion, diced
- ½ cup of panko bread crumb
- 2 pounds of ground beef and pork
- ½ tbsp. of soy sauce
- 2 cups of dashi
- ½ tsp. of salt

- ½ tsp. of pepper
- 1 tsp. of grated ginger, ground

Directions

Boil your cabbage leaves for about 10 minutes. When it cools, remove the limp leaves and microwave them then add back with the other leaves, drain and trim out the stems from the leaves in a v-shape way.

Chop the stems and mix with all your other ingredients asides the leaves. Roll the mixture in your palm and make about 10 balls. Place balls on the end of each leaf and wrap. Fill your pan with Dashi, place the leaf balls in it and cook for about 20 minutes.

Remove from heat, drain the dashi and let it cool before packing.

Green beans coated in pine nuts

Fried pine nuts give your nuts a different and amazing taste. If you make this for your kids during lunch, they will long for more.

Preparation Time: 10 minutes

Makes: 2

Ingredients

- 1 tbsp. of pine nuts
- 1 cup of green beans
- ½ tbsp. of white miso, mild
- 1 tsp. of butter

Directions

Put your pine nuts in a small non-stick pan and heat on high heat for about 3 minutes or until it is toasted lightly. Remove nuts from the pan and set aside. Tail the green beans, chop into pieces and place it in the pan.

Add water to the pan and cook until the beans become tender and crispy. Drain the excess water and return the green beans to the pan, add your miso and butter and stir until it is heated through.

Add the pine nuts, mix properly and pack in your bento box.

Sweet white beans

If you don't have white beans, you can use haricot instead. Combining your white beans with honey and sugar gives it the right glossy look and it is a very filling meal for your bento box.

Preparation Time: 90 minutes

Makes: 2

Ingredients

- 2 cups of white beans, dry
- ½ tsp. of baking soda
- 1 tsp. of honey
- ½ cup of sugar
- 1 tbsp. of soy sauce

Directions

Soak your beans overnight in water. Drain the liquid and boil in another clean water. When the bean is boiled, drain the water and fill water in another pot. Add the beans and baking soda and simmer for another 40 minutes or until the beans is soft.

Add sugar and honey and cook for another 30 minutes, add soy sauce and simmer for extra few minutes, remove and dish in your bento box.

White rice and peas

You need to have your white rice pre-cooked a night before, then you can prepare an amazing lunch from the rice together with your peas.

Preparation Time: 10 minutes

Makes: 2

Ingredients

- 1 tbsp. of frozen green peas
- 1 cup of pre-cooked rice
- ½ tsp. of salt
- 2 cups of water

Directions

Put your peas in a bowl and add a little salt. Add water to the peas, cover with a plastic wrap and place in a microwave for a few minutes.

Mix the peas with the rice and serve.

Fried spinach

Fried spinach and corn is a meal that is easy to make and you can always pair it with your mushroom rice and any vegetable of your choice.

Preparation Time: 10 minutes

Makes: 1

Ingredients

- 1 can of frozen spinach
- 1 cup of corn
- 1 tsp. of ground black pepper
- 1 tbsp. of butter
- 1 tsp. of sea salt

Directions

Melt your butter in a pan, add the corn and spinach and simmer until it is wilted. Add your pepper and salt and simmer for 1 minute.

Remove and let it cool before placing in your bento box.

Baked tomato with pesto

Ever tasted baked cherry tomatoes? It makes a great sauce that you can always mix with your rice or pasta.

Preparation Time: 30 minutes

Makes: 1

Ingredients

- 4 ripe cherry tomatoes
- 1 tbsp. of pesto sauce
- 1 tsp. of parmesan cheese, grated

Directions

Cut your tomatoes in half and arrange on a foil, cover with your pesto sauce and sprinkle your cheese on it. Place in your toaster oven and bake for about 10 minutes. Or when it begins to bubble, remove and let it cool a bit before placing it in your bento box.

Bunny shaped apple

Do you want to pack lunch in a bento box for your kids? Then making it colorful will make them love it. Shaped apples are perfect for your kids.

Preparation Time: 10 minutes

Makes: 6

Ingredients

- 1 pound of apples
- 2 cups of water
- ½ tsp. of salt

Directions

Cut your apple into 6, remove the core and mark a V shape on the skin with a sharp knife. Peel off the park that is marked, including the excess apple, add the bunnies in salted water and keep. Remove from water and pack in your bento box for your kids.

Mini hamburgers wrapped in bacon

Hamburgers made with bacon are one healthy meal that you should not joke with. It is tasty and the maple syrup makes it more amazing.

Preparation Time: 15 minutes

Makes: 20

Ingredients

- 10 slices of bacon, halved
- 2 tbsp. of maple syrup
- ½ cup of oil
- 20 mini burger buns

Directions

Wrap your hamburger in half slice of your bacon, place in your pan and fry until your bacon is crispy. Drain the fat away from the pan, add your maple syrup and turn the hamburger until it is caramelized. Remove and serve.

Shrimp shuumai dumpling

You can get shuumai skin in a store, although the meal takes a little time to prepare, but it is very tasty and filling.

Preparation Time: 70 minutes

Makes: 10

Ingredients

- 2 pounds of Shrimp, chopped
- 1 tbsp. of Mirin,
- 1 Medium sized onion, chopped
- 1 tbsp. of Soy sauce
- 1 tbsp. of Cornstarch
- 1 tsp. of Sesame oil
- 4 pounds of Ground pork

- 1 tsp. of Ginger
- 1 tsp. of Ground black pepper
- 1 tsp. of Salt
- 1 pound of Shuumari skin dumplings

Directions

Place your pork in a bowl, and add your cornstarch, mirin, and ginger. Stir properly until you get a fine paste, then add your shrimps and onions, a little salt and pepper and stir.

Fill the center of each of your shuumai skin with your filling and seal tightly so it doesn't fall out. Slightly grease your steamer and place your shuumai in it, simmer for about 15 minutes.

Remove and serve in your bento box.

Spicy pork hamburger

Mini-hamburgers can be made as much as you want and it is very tasty and healthy. Perfect for you and your family.

Preparation Time: 10 minutes

Makes: 20

Ingredients

- 1 pound of ground pork
- 1 tsp. of fresh grated ginger
- 1 tbsp. of chopped coriander leaves
- ½ cup of hot chili sauce
- 20 burger bun
- 2 tbsp. of oil

Directions

Mix your pork, ginger, and coriander leaves in a bowl. Heat oil in a pan and place mixture in it, simmer for a few minute, remove and place in one side of the burger buns and cover with the other end.

Place in your bento box to be enjoyed later.

Ham and cheese veggies

You can decide to make this a night before you need it. It is tasty and healthy.

Preparation Time: 30 minutes

Makes: 2

Ingredients

- 1 small carrot, peeled and sliced long
- 1 can of green beans
- ½ tsp. of salt
- 2 slices of ham
- 2 tbsp. of softened cream cheese
- 2 cups of water

Directions

Boil a little water in a pan, add a little salt, place your carrot and green beans and cook for about 5 minutes or until it is tender and crispy. Drain and set aside to cool, drain under cold water, dry with a paper towel, and set aside.

Set aside about 2 strips of carrot and few green beans then chop the rest. Place plastic wrap on your table, place the ham on the plastic, spread cheese on it, place your carrot and green beans, roll the ham firm. Place in your fridge overnight.

Unwrap in the morning cut into pieces and serve in your bento box.

Shrimp wrapped in garlic

Shrimp in garlic gives it a unique taste and like you know, shrimp is an amazingly healthy meal and it is perfect for a healthy lunch. You can pair it with rice or French fries.

Preparation Time: 15 minutes

Makes: 2

Ingredients

- 1 tsp. of garlic oil
- 2 packs of frozen shrimp
- ½ tsp. of salt
- ½ tsp. of ground black pepper

Directions

Heat your garlic oil in a pan over medium heat, add your frozen shrimp and simmer until it is no longer pink. Add your salt and pepper and simmer for a few more minutes. Remove and serve with your rice.

Lemon flavored celeriac and carrot salad

This salad can last longer if kept in the fridge. It goes with any protein of your choice and you can always pack it in your bento box to have during lunch.

Preparation Time: 15 minutes
Makes: 6
Ingredients

- 1 big peeled celeriac
- 2 big carrots
- 1 tbsp. of lemon juice
- ½ tsp. of salt
- 1 tsp. of black pepper
- 1btsp. of sugar
- 1 tbsp. of oil

Directions

Slice your celeriac and carrot into thin shreds using a grater. Place the shredded veggies in a bowl, add your other ingredients, with your salt and pepper, let it rest a little in your bento box before feasting on it.

Conclusion

When it comes to packing your bento box, adding fruits and veggies should be made necessary. Eating lunch with fruits is very healthy and nutritious. Hence, with these 30 recipes, you can never run out of ideas of the kind of meals to pack in your bento boxes. Get rid of unhealthy junks for lunch by quickly fixing lunch and packing it in your bento box.

Don't miss out!

Visit the website below and you can sign up to receive emails whenever Ida Smith publishes a new book. There's no charge and no obligation.

https://books2read.com/r/B-A-LRXL-PSGSB

BOOKS 2 READ

Connecting independent readers to independent writers.

www.ingramcontent.com/pod-product-compliance
Ingram Content Group UK Ltd.
Pitfield, Milton Keynes, MK11 3LW, UK
UKHW061655190726
13853UKWH00008B/2215

9 798201 176976